THE CATHEDRAL CI

ST DEIN

The Dean's Welcome

Welcome to the Cathedral Church of St Deiniol. About the year 525AD a man named Deiniol founded a cell on this site. In about 546AD he was made Bishop and given spiritual oversight of the then Gwynedd, by Maelgwn, Prince of Gwynedd. His church became a cathedral and the area a diocese, perhaps the oldest territorial diocese in the United Kingdom.

Much of the present building dates from the 14th century, but it is no anachronism; it has much of historic interest, but it is no museum; it thrills, but it does not overawe. For nearly 1,500 years this has been, and still is, a 'house of God'; a place where there is a daily offering of true worship and praise to the glory of God. For this it was built, and for this we strive to maintain it.

The Dean and Chapter welcome you and pray that your visit may bring you inspiration and peace.

Early History

BELOW:
The presbytery looking east, with the Bishop's Throne, which dates from 1879, on the right. The elegant ceiling was designed by Sir George Gilbert Scott.

The Cathedral Church of Bangor occupies one of the most ancient ecclesiastical sites in Great Britain. Deiniol, the founder of the see, was consecrated Bishop in around 546AD, some 20 years after he had established his first cell on the site. A man of noble birth, he had been educated in Wales with other young men including Maelgwn, son of the King of Gwynedd, and it can be safely assumed that it was Maelgwn who gave Deiniol the land on which he built his church and dwelling place. Deiniol enclosed his land by driving posts into the ground and weaving branches between them.

The name Bangor, when used as a common noun, denotes 'the binding part of a wattle fence', and the site of the monastery at Bangor took its name from the wattle enclosure surrounding it. While the other monasteries of the same

name were called Bangor in honour of the first and most famous, our Bangor became the 'Bangor Fawr yn Arfon' and 'Bennchor moer in Britannia' of the Welsh and Irish chronicles. Some years ago the marks of what may have been a very early church were uncovered at Llandygái, about a mile south of Bangor – an oblong building measuring 14ft by 10ft constructed of vertical posts. Deiniol's first church may have been something similar. We do not know how many times this was rebuilt during the next 400 years or when stone replaced wood for building; no remains of a pre-Norman church are visible above ground in Wales.

LEFT: ⑤
'Christ the King' (on the north wall of the presbytery) is one of seven statues of Flemish origin in the cathedral. They were probably thrown out in the 17th century but were found and restored in 1961.

History Chart

c. **525**	St Deiniol built his first cell on the site.
c. **546**	St Deiniol consecrated Bishop and his church became a cathedral.
547	Death of Maelgwn, King of Gwynedd.
c. **572**	Death of St Deiniol.
631	Bangor Fawr in Britain burnt according to *The Annals of Ulster.*
1073	Vikings robbed and burnt the church.
c. **1100**	Gruffudd regained his kingdom, Gwynedd.
c. **1130**	Gruffudd and Bishop David rebuilt the cathedral in stone.
1210	Cathedral destroyed by King John's men.
c. **1275**	South transept completed.
c. **1300**	East end and north transept completed. Small Lady Chapel added.
1309	The central tower burnt down.
c. **1300**–*c.* **1350**	Nave extended to its present size.
1402	Cathedral destroyed in the Glyndŵr rebellion.
1480	Rebuilding began in earnest.
1510–30	Present arcade and clerestory built.
1532	Western tower completed.
1870–80	Restoration by Sir George Gilbert Scott.
1966–67	Central tower completed with battlements and pyramidical cap.

We do know, however, that the church was destroyed by the Vikings in 1073. With the Normans pressing from the east and native rulers pressing from the south, it is unlikely that any rebuilding was undertaken until Gruffudd ap Cynan (died 1137) had regained his kingdom of Gwynedd, defeated his enemies and restored order. The earliest surviving structures are of the church built in the time of Bishop David (1120–39): these consist of a round-headed window (completely filled in) and a plain buttress, in the south wall of the presbytery, east of the south transept. The Norman cathedral ended here, in an apse, the chord of the apse coinciding almost exactly with the present step at the east end of the choir. This building may have been destroyed when King John's men burnt Bangor in 1210.

Destruction and Rebuilding

Gruffudd ap Cynan, died 1137, King of North Wales. His coat of arms can be seen on the Precentor's Stall. Gruffudd ap Cynan, father of Owain Gwynedd, was buried in a place of honour, on the north side of the high altar.

Owain Gwynedd, died 1170, Prince of North Wales. His coat of arms can be seen on the Canon-in-Residence's Stall. It is known that Owain Gwynedd was buried on the south side of the high altar of the Norman church, slightly west of where the Bishop's Throne now stands.

Llywelyn ap Iorwerth (Llywelyn the Great), Prince of North Wales 1196–1240. His coat of arms can be seen on the Dean's Stall. He was the grandson of Owain Gwynedd.

ABOVE: ⑦
The coats of arms on the Chapter Stalls are those of medieval benefactors of the church and local tribes. They also include those of three of the Princes of North Wales, shown here.

At the end of the 13th century Bishop Anian I (1267–1305) removed the apse and built the presbytery to its present extent, with a square end; he also rebuilt the crossing, enlarged the south transept to its present size, removing the apse and adding a Lady Chapel. The small buttress under the south transept window belongs to this period.

The north transept was probably extended after 1300, possibly in the time of Anian II (Anian Sais, 1309–28) who removed the apse and added a chapel dedicated to St John the Baptist and St John the Evangelist. A vestry and chapter house were added on the north side of the presbytery, and the chancel paved with tiles. The tower on the crossing was burnt in 1309 and was not rebuilt.

During the 14th century rebuilding continued westward, the aisled nave having an arcade of seven bays (not six as today). The aisle windows indicate a date early in the century while the moulding of the doorways belongs to the middle of the century. Rebuilding may have been slow; certain differences in style suggest the south aisle was built some time before the north aisle. The church suffered again in 1402, during the rebellion of Owain Glyndŵr, and although the extent of the destruction is not known, subsequent rebuilding suggests the transepts and nave arcades may have been ruined. The Lady Chapel was never rebuilt.

Credit for the work which commenced towards the end of the 15th century is generally given to Bishop Dean (1496–1500), credit which perhaps belongs rightly to Richard Kyffin, Dean of Bangor (1480–1502). According to the Welsh poet Guto'r Glyn, Kyffin repaired the choir and roofed at least part of the church with lead, probably the choir and presbytery. In order to provide more light for the choir, now moved from the crossing to the presbytery, six windows were either opened or enlarged, all filled with painted glass, and at least four naming the donors: on the south side of the presbytery a window depicting Saints Catherine and Dwynwen, the gift of Dean Kyffin, and the middle window with 'a picture of S. Deiniol' the gift of Dr Maurice Glyn; two of the windows on the north side were given by the Penrhyn family of Llandygái. The east window dates from *c.*1500, and according to tradition was the gift of the Llwydiarth family of Llannerch-y-medd, Anglesey. The frame was carefully repaired by John Cooper of Beaumaris in 1785.

Under Bishop Skevington (1509–33), who was also Abbot of Beaulieu, a new nave arcade of six bays was built, and a clerestory with corresponding six windows added; the transept windows were reshaped, and the large window in the south wall of the sanctuary added. Finally the western tower was built, the Latin inscription above the door testifying that 'Thomas Skevington, Bishop of Bangor, had this bell-tower and Church built in the year of the Virgin's giving birth, 1532'. Early in the 18th century the medieval chapter room and vestry north of the presbytery were extended eastwards and a library built above; this upper storey was redesigned and rebuilt 1776–81.

LEFT: ⑧
Gilbert Scott had copies made of three of the early 14th-century tiles which were found during the 19th-century restoration and these can be seen on the floor of the chancel and the Lady Chapel. Shown here is an eagle with two heads, clutching fish. The fish was an early Christian symbol. Medieval people believed this was the emblem of the tribe of Coel Hen, the tribe to which Deiniol belonged. They were Christians early on.

LEFT: ⑧
A peculiar bird which may be the 'caladrius', a bird which supposedly visited the room of a sick man. If the bird looked at the man he would recover; if it did not, the man would die.

RIGHT: ⑧
A rabbit with a bow and arrow; 'hunting the hunter' was a popular theme.

19th-Century Restoration

LEFT:
The pastoral staff or crozier presented to the Bishop at his Installation is the one bequeathed by Humphrey Humphreys, Bishop of Bangor 1689–1701.

During the early 19th century the population of Bangor increased rapidly and several attempts were made to provide more seating capacity, and also to cater for the English immigrants. Sir George Gilbert Scott described the work as 'the most execrable gimcrack that ever disgraced a Church'. Dean James Vincent (1862–76) decided on a radical restoration.

On the advice of Sir George Gilbert Scott, it was decided to restore or partially reconstruct the choir, transepts and chapter house 'in such style as is indicated by their few remaining fragments'. He found sufficient bases of the 14th-century crossing arches, and sufficient fragments of arches and capitals to be able to reconstruct the 14th-century crossing; sufficient fragments of window frames and tracery to reconstruct the transept windows of Anian's day; and sufficient fragments of masonry to enable him to reconstruct the 14th-century buttresses on the south transept and east end. The arches from the aisles to the transepts were re-opened, and the chancel and Lady Chapel (the south transept) were floored with replicas of some of the medieval tiles found in the debris under the floor.

For lack of funds Scott had to abandon the idea of building the lofty central tower and spire. His tower rose no higher than the ridge of the roofs, a mere stump. In 1945 a bequest was made by A.D. King of Caernarfon for the erection of a central tower, but engineers doubted whether the foundations, owing to subsidence, would bear even a modified spire. Later, 1966–67, the stump of Scott's central tower was finished off with battlements and a pyramidical cap.

The Bangor Pontifical

RIGHT:
An illustrated page from the famous Bangor Pontifical, *which dates from the late 13th or early 14th century, shows a bishop consecrating a church. The* Pontifical *is now kept in the Library of the University College, Bangor.*

FAR RIGHT:
The musical notes that accompany part of the liturgy are proof that choral services were held in the cathedral at this time. This is one of the earliest known examples of a service book containing musical notes. A plate from the Pontifical.

LEFT: (10)
The stained glass window in the south aisle which depicts St Deiniol (centre) flanked by St Dyfrig (died c.502), bishop and missionary in south-east Wales, and St Beuno (died c.642), the last of the great native saints, with churches dedicated in his name in Powys, Clwyd and Gwynedd. Beuno was not a bishop; according to tradition the early saints carried croziers, with which they often performed miracles.

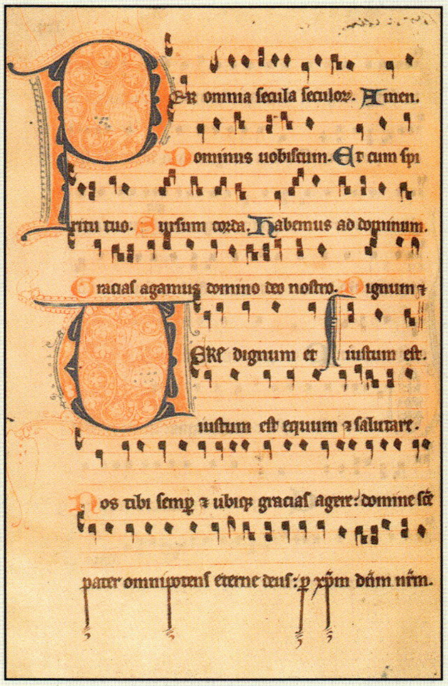

Bishop Anian's Pontifical

Bangor Cathedral can boast of a rich and varied library of over 4,500 volumes, now deposited for safety at the Library of the University College. Its greatest treasure is Bishop Anian's *Pontifical*, which dates from at least the early years of the 14th century. It is written on vellum, rubricated (with headings) in red and blue, with illuminations inlaid with gold leaf and bordered in blue, green and black.

A pontifical is a book containing those services which only a bishop can perform, such as Confirmation, Ordination and Consecration of churches. There were two bishops of Bangor named Anian: Anian who held the see from 1267–1305, and Anian Sais (Anian who could speak English), 1309–28. The older and more traditional view of the book is that it belonged to the former of the two bishops; later scholars suggested that it was compiled for the use of Anian Sais, but the present archivist, relying on marginalia, favours Anian I. It has an interesting history; it has survived the ravages of war probably by being removed to safe keeping when danger seemed imminent. It was lost after the Owain Glyndŵr rebellion but was returned to the Cathedral by Bishop Ednam in 1485, and it was returned again in 1701 by Bishop Humphreys. From 1939 to 1945 it shared with some of Britain's most historic treasures the sanctuary of the tunnels beneath the National Library of Wales at Aberystwyth. It was returned from its third exile on 11th April, 1946.

The Lady Chapel

On the west wall of the south transept, now the Lady Chapel, are plaques commemorating two Welsh poets: Goronwy Owen (1723–69), a Welsh poet of note, exercised a permanent influence on Welsh poetry. His first curacy was in his native Anglesey then, after ten years in England, he emigrated to Virginia in 1757. While a pupil at Friars School, Bangor, he was obliged to attend early morning service daily at the cathedral, the grammar school pupils occupying this transept or the crossing.

Edmund Prys (1544–1623), Rector of Maentwrog and Archdeacon of Merioneth, composed his metrical psalms in a metre better adapted for setting to music than any previous attempts in Welsh. His published work, bound with the 1621 Prayer Book, included a number of tunes, the first Welsh book in which music was printed. Many of his metrical psalms are still sung today.

Tradition has identified the arched tomb in the south wall as that of Owain Gwynedd (died 1170) and that of Bishop Hywel ap Gronw (died *c.*1373). Neither can be accepted; the style, late 13th century, is too early for that of the bishop, while this part of the cathedral was not built until about 1275. The broken slab, with floriated cross, now on the tomb, appears not to belong to it. The small broken crucifix, affixed to the rear wall of the tomb, the figure hanging from the cross bar with arms almost vertical, head inclined to the right, belongs to the 14th or early 15th century. A similar crucifix can be seen in the panelling behind the altar of the Lady Chapel.

The painting above the altar was executed by Brian Thomas and depicts the appearance of the Risen Lord to the two disciples at Emmaus. The Risen Lord alone is draped in the familiar conventional robes of the East; the beckoning figures at a typical British doorway present the appearance in the context of present-day life and suggest its relevance for all times. The painting, in memory of Griffith Roberts, Dean of Bangor from 1903 to 1934, was presented by his family, and dedicated on St David's Day, 1955.

The arch framing the picture was discovered and restored during Scott's restoration. Originally it formed the entrance into the Lady Chapel built by Bishop Anian I, destroyed in 1402, and never rebuilt. The reredos was designed by Alban Caroe, and erected in 1950 by

ABOVE:
The arch framing the mural over the altar of the Lady Chapel was the entrance into the original Lady Chapel built by Anian I. It was destroyed in 1402 and never rebuilt.

Margaret Henrietta Watts, in memory of her parents and family. South of the altar is a plaque in memory of the late J.C. Jones, Bishop of Bangor (1949–56), beloved by all. The glass in the south window was presented in memory of H.T. Edwards, Dean of Bangor (1876–84), whose memorial plaque may be seen on the north side of the altar.

BELOW: ⑨
The mural of Christ and the two persons on the road to Emmaus painted by Brian Thomas in 1955, above the altar in the Lady Chapel.

The windows in the south aisle depict Celtic saints, most of them closely associated with the evangelization of North Wales in the 6th and 7th centuries. The Lectern was presented in 1905 by the family of Evan Lewis, Dean of Bangor (1884–1901), an eminent ecclesiastic who strove vigorously and successfully to propagate the principles and practices of the Oxford Movement in his diocese. He assisted in the production of a Welsh Hymn Book and a Welsh Gregorian Psalter. On the floor near the Lectern is a stone commemorating two rulers of Gwynedd: Gruffudd ap Cynan (died 1137) and his son, Owain Gwynedd (died 1170). On the south wall, to the east of the door, are several memorials including two to former bishops of Bangor. The screen at the end of the aisle was erected in 1960. It bears the mark of the 'mouse man' Robert Thompson (1876–1955) of Kilburn, Yorkshire, who carved a mouse on every piece of work he executed.

RIGHT:
Today's choristers, 'descendants' of the exceptionally sweet singers, who had no equal, that the poet Dafydd ap Gwilym heard when he visited the cathedral in the mid-14th century. He was also impressed by the fine new organ.

The Nave

RIGHT: ⑪
The early 15th-century octagonal font of fine yellow sandstone. Only one of the heraldic shields around the stem (on the left), that of the See of Bangor, has been identified.

The first thing you may have observed within the cathedral is the curious lack of symmetry in the details of nave and aisles. The tower arch is not opposite the middle of the nave but slightly to the north of it. The south aisle windows are higher from the floor than those of the north aisle, and their internal arches are differently treated; also below them, a string course runs the whole length of the wall, a feature lacking on the north wall. The southern pillars of the nave are not exactly opposite the northern, but slightly to the east of them. The nave has only six arches and six clerestory windows to match seven openings in the aisle walls (six windows and a doorway). To compensate for the loss of the one bay, projecting walls were built out at both ends of the nave: the old 13th-century 'take off' is distinctly visible near the south side of the tower arch. The north and south doorways are not on the same level, the former being as much below the level of the nave floor as the latter is above it. At one time the floors of the north aisle and north transept were three or four feet below the level of the remainder of the cathedral.

BELOW:
The fine reredos of 1881 was designed by Oldrid Scott, son of Sir George Gilbert Scott. It was partially restored and gilded in 1984.

The present arrangement of the interior dates from Sir George Gilbert Scott's restoration. Before 1824 the choir stalls were in what is now the presbytery and the chancel occupied only half its present area. The Welsh parochial services were held in the transepts and crossing, the pulpit and reading desk being placed near the present Dean's stall. With the restoration begun in 1825 a stone screen was placed in the fifth bay from the west. The Welsh congregation was accommodated in the four western bays, with the altar in front of the screen, the reading desk on the north side and the pulpit on the south side. The English congregation and choir occupied the eastern part; the choir was moved to the first bay, and the organ built against the screen, while the congregation sat in the transepts and presbytery. This order lasted until Scott's restoration, and old prints of the interior may be seen in the museum corner.

The three western windows of painted glass, by David Evans of Shrewsbury, are regarded as fine examples of the art of their time. Originally placed by Dean Cotton in the east window (1838) they were moved to their present positions by Scott, one light being jettisoned. The figures depicted are: *north aisle*: Peter, John, Paul; *western tower*: Aaron, Moses, King David; *south aisle*: Matthew, Mark and Luke.

On the wall west of the font may be seen memorials to three bishops, while on the north wall, opposite the font, may be seen the Mostyn Christ. This almost life-sized carved oak figure, representing Christ at Calvary, has been entrusted to the custody of the Dean and Chapter of Bangor Cathedral by Lord Mostyn of Mostyn Hall, Clwyd. The figure is seated on a rock; the feet are closely shackled by a rope, which also bound the hands, but these are now lost, together with the whole of the right arm and the left forearm. The crown of thorns is worn, and the attitude and expression betoken extreme weariness and exhaustion, 'a man of sorrows, and acquainted with grief'. As there are no stigmata it must represent the last moments before the actual crucifixion.

ABOVE:
The Rood hanging above the choir screen was designed by Alban Caroe and dates from 1950.

LEFT: (13)
The almost life-size carved wooden figure of Christ at Calvary is known as The Mostyn Christ *and dates from the late 15th or early 16th century.*

The figure belongs to the late 15th or early 16th century; examples of this type, known as a Bound Rood, are extremely rare in Wales. Judging from the detailed description given by a contemporary poet, it may well be the effigy set up in the garden of Rhuddlan Priory in 1518. After dissolution the priory fell into the hands of a recusant branch of the Mostyn family, that of Talacre, who intermarried with another recusant family, Pugh of Penrhyn Creuddyn (between Colwyn Bay and Llandudno), who sheltered priests and a secret printing press. The figure may have been brought there for secret worship, eventually finding a

LEFT: ②
On the screen at the end of the north aisle can be seen the 'mouse mark' of Robert Thompson the craftsman (1876–1955). There is another mouse on the screen at the end of the south aisle near the entrance to the Lady Chapel.

LEFT: ⑭
A modern interpretation of the Crucifixion by Margaret Cross, 1968, who was a student at St Mary's College of Education in Bangor.

BELOW:
An old print showing the cathedral and city market in around 1800.

home at Gloddaith, one of the Mostyn mansions in the area.

In the museum corner, west of the north door, are various items of interest. Three misericords are all that survive of the cathedral's early woodwork and one can be seen here. Also to be seen is a Charter given to Friars School, Bangor, 1561, which bears the seal of Queen Elizabeth I. Geoffrey Glyn, an Anglesey man, brother of William Glyn the last Catholic Bishop of Bangor (1555–58), acquired in 1553 the lands and buildings of the suppressed Bangor Friary; when he died in 1557 he left this property and an additional endowment for the foundation of a grammar school. Letters Patent issued in 1561 made the Dean and Chapter its governing body.

Affixed to the west wall is a sepulchral slab dating from the 14th century and known as the 'Eva slab' from the inscription: 'Here lies Eva who was the wife of . . . anwel on whose soul may (God) have mercy'. The effigy depicts a lady robed in late 14th-century garments from whose left hand hangs a rosary to which are fastened three rings and two brooches of the type called Pilgrim brooches. The

ABOVE:
The six cathedrals of the Church in Wales in their geographical setting, one of two murals painted by Brian Thomas. The other portrays some of the great names in the history of the Welsh Church.

slab came from the chapel on the north side of the presbytery. The 13th-century stone coffin was discovered at the old Dominican Friary and recovered from an Anglesey farm and placed in the cathedral in 1980.

Among the sundry stones are a fragment bearing fourcord plait work, and the arm of a Celtic cross, both dating back to the 10th century and the pre-Norman church. A fragment of a semi-octagonal shaft ornamented with a chevron belongs to the Norman period, and the mutilated stone crucifix to the 15th century. The medieval tiles were found in the debris under the chancel floor and belong to the early 14th-century church. The tiles, depicting animals and birds, are unique to Bangor.

It is our sincere hope that you have enjoyed your visit, for we are proud of our cathedral where prayer and praise to God are still offered – both in Welsh and English – and where pilgrims and visitors are always welcome. May the blessing and peace of God go with you.

Acknowledgements

Text © The Dean and Chapter, Bangor Cathedral.

Designed by John Buckley.

Edited by Ann Lockhart.

All photographs are © Pitkin Pictorials (by Peter Smith of Newbery Smith Associates) except for:
Page 1: Aerofilms
Page 9 (bottom): The Reverend Dewi James
Page 12 (bottom right): Bangor Cathedral

Printed in Great Britain by Cedar Colour, Eastleigh, Hants.
ISBN 0 85372 723 6 194/10

A view of the cathedral, showing the be[illegible]wer built in 1532.

£2.00

PITKIN

ISBN 0-85372-723-6